NIGEL'S WRIST

Nigel's Wrist

Nicholas Corder

J. Garnet Miller

First published by J. Garnet Miller
(A division of Cressrelles Publishing Company Limited)
10 Station Road Industrial Estate, Colwall, Near Malvern, WR13 6RN
Telephone/Fax: (01684) 540154

A CIP record for this book is available from the British Library.

ISBN: 0-85343-638-X

Printed in the UK by Cressrelles Publishing Company Ltd.

Characters

Nigel Struthers

- a postgraduate student in his early to mid twenties

(Dennis Herdman)

Nurse Rogers

- a female nurse of similar age

(Cleo Barnham)

The professional cast for the production at the Theatre by the Lake in Keswick, directed by Ian Forrest, in November 2001, are listed after each character entry.

Scene

The action is continuous and takes place in the sperm bank of an unnamed National Health Service clinic.

The set is wonderfully, affordably bare save for a set of curtain screens on castors of the type you find in clinics and hospitals, and a medical couch. There is no need for any kind of clever lighting, although if Nigel were to be isolated in a pool of light during some of his monologues, this might work well. During the moments of national pride, a gobo of the Union Jack works well.

Properties/costume required: sample bottle (empty); clipboard; feather duster; riding crop. Typical student clothing for Nigel and a nurse's uniform, white coat, riding outfit and French maid's outfit for Nurse.

The play would benefit from music where indicated, but again this is not wholly necessary if it creates a technical problem.

Running Time - 30 minutes

Act I

Music - "We're only Making Plans for Nigel" by XTC

Nigel is barely visible behind the screens. Only when he stands erect can we see his head and shoulders. He is talking to himself.

Nigel: Come on then, little feller. Let's rise to the occasion. Come on. I need a little help, here. *(As Bogart.)* "You did it for her, now do it for me." *(Himself.)* Come on, now. A little drum roll *(imitates a paradiddle)* and up, up, up, up. No? Nothing doing? *(Barrow boy.)* "Come on, my son, we need the money. You're all that stands between me and a night on the piss." *(Himself.)* 'Stands', that's a joke.

Nigel zips up and comes front of screen to address the audience.

Nigel: It's not fair is it? You can't stop it. It doesn't matter where you are, it takes over. You're in a lecture on hyper-inflation in inter-war Germany and it hyper-inflates of its own accord. You're watching a programme about state corruption in Namibia and the next thing you know, your trousers can hardly take the strain. It's almost as though the more boring something is, the more it does its own thing. Watch the Trooping of the Colour and Count Zeppelin's nipping round to take a plaster cast as a model for his next venture.

I may have something there - *Struthers' Rule of Direct Erectile - Boredom Co-efficient.* Complete lack of action and reaction are equal and opposite.

1

(*Pompous Swede.*) "And this year's Nobel Physics Prize goes to Nigel Struthers for his seminal work on blood flow and tedium." (*As though accepting an award.*) "Thank you, thank you. And may I say that things are so interesting here in Sweden that I have difficulty containing myself." (*Himself.*) Perhaps that's the secret. Think boring thoughts.

Nigel goes back behind the screen.

Nigel (*As a hypnotist*): "You are feeling bored. You will think only boring thoughts. Bore you stupid. Bore you rigid. Your thoughts are getting tedious, stuffy, leaden. Conservative Party Conference... the Turner Prize... Arsenal Football Club... Celine Dion and on and on and on ... Radio 2 ... commuters ... people who vote ecology ... shaving ..." (*Himself.*) Yes, that's a little better! (*Hypnotist.*) "... people in pubs who have their own tankards .. . *The South Bank Show*." (*As Frankie Howerd.*) "Oo-er, Missus, a little bit of rhyming slang there for you." (*Hypnotist.*) "...Gordon Brown... Morris dancing... Ronan Keating... the periodic table ... the *Daily Telegraph* letters page ... the Space Shuttle." (*A fake US accent.*) "Five ... four ... three ... two ... one ... we have lift off!"

*Enter **Nurse**.*

Nurse: Have you got someone else in there, Mr Struthers?

Nigel (*American*): "Houston, we have a problem."

Nurse: I thought I heard a man's voice.

Nigel: You did. It was mine.

Nurse: Only you come across all sorts of stories. Apparently, they'll do it almost anywhere. Even in public toilets.

Nigel: Who will?

Nurse (*Conspiratorially*): Men.

Nigel (*As Spock*): "It's life, Jim, but not as we know it."

Nurse: Are you sure you haven't got anyone in there with you? It's only one per cubicle.

Nigel: Why don't you look for yourself?

Nurse: I couldn't do that, Mr Struthers. It would be improper.

Nigel: Improper?

Nurse: Unprofessional. Unladylike.

Nigel: You spend your working life giving out little bottles to men who then... *(Unsure how far he can take this line of thought, he stops.)*

Nurse: It's not the path I'd have chosen.

Nigel: Don't tell me. It was either this or urban terrorism.

Nurse: It seems I'm here because of a clerical error.

Nigel *(To audience)*: As the vicar's bastard son said to the Bishop. *(To Nurse.)* Ain't nobody here but us chicken neck wringers.

Nigel moves in front of the screen.

Nurse: I wanted to work in gynaecology.

Nigel: Didn't we all.

Nurse: There's no need to be facetious, Mr Struthers. It's not funny when your ambitions are thwarted.

Nigel: You're telling me.

Nurse: What d'you mean?

Nigel: Well ... I ...

Nurse: Not behaving himself, the little chap?

Nigel: You make him sound like a naughty schoolboy. No. You know what I mean ... it just won't ... I've been trying for ages.

Nurse: Have you tried letting your mind go blank? After all, you're a man. It shouldn't be too much of a problem.

Nigel: Oh, good idea! Sarcasm! Very encouraging! That's *exactly* what I *was* doing.

Nurse: Perhaps you weren't letting your mind go quite blank enough.

Nigel: Blank is blank. You can't have degrees of blankness. Something's either blank or it isn't. It's like being quite unique. It is or it isn't unique.

Nurse: Calm down, Mr Struthers.

Nigel: How can I when ... this ...

Nurse: It happens to lots of men.

Nigel: Yes, but they're probably middle-aged. I'm young. I have my prostate.

Nurse: I'm telling you, it happens to everyone.

Nigel: No, nurse, it doesn't happen to everyone. It doesn't happen to women and it doesn't happen to me.

Nurse: Now you're nit-picking. True, it may not happen to women . . .

Nigel: There's no may about it . . . You did do a nursing course, didn't you? Women have a slightly different anatomy. Perhaps they told you that. Or were you off the day they did vaso-congestion?

Nurse: Obviously I have studied this kind of thing. It was on the syllabus. There was a rather unpleasant picture with much more detail than was strictly necessary on page ninety-three. I was just trying to point out that apparently it's commoner than you think. A lot of you men experience this kind of difficulty...

Nigel: Well, I don't.

Nurse: Especially at moments of great stress.

Nigel (*Shouting*)**:** I am not stressed!

Nurse: There's no need to get excited.

Nigel: There's every need to get excited. Getting excited is what it's all about.

Nurse (*Conciliatory*)**:** Would you like me to bring you some magazines? It might help. Many of the gentlemen who come here to . . . to . . . do find that a magazine . . . Some of our donors find that a magazine can aid the process.

Nigel: I'm sorry, Nurse. No, I don't want a magazine. I'm just a little edgy. Nothing I can't handle. I thought it would be easier than this.

Nurse: Some things in life are harder than we imagine, Mr Struthers.

Nigel: Ha, ha. The apposite phrase as ever.

Nurse: It's not easy for me either. Ugly things they are - all veiny and knobbly. Not like the female form. I wanted to deal with women.

Nigel: All very interesting, I'm sure, but it's not getting us anywhere is it? Frankly, Nurse, I need the money.

Nurse: You're not the only one.

Nigel: Yes, but your wages don't depend on whether you can do it or not. If I can't get something into this little bottle, I simply don't get paid. You can't cheat, you know. They'll soon find out. You can't just sneak a bit of yoghurt in and pass it off as the real thing.

Nurse: Really!

Nigel: Imagine it all nine months down the line. Congratulations, Mrs Smith, you've just given birth to a low-calorie, firm-set, peach melba flavour dessert.

Nurse: You're wrong, Mr Struthers. This is the new National Health Service. We're talking government targets.

Nigel: Like zero emissions, I suppose.

Nurse: It's spreadsheets not bed sheets. Achievement indicators and performance-related pay.

Nigel: What's the prize then? A teasmaid? A wok? A weekend for two in Skegness? What carrot do they dangle?

Nurse: I'd rather you didn't talk about dangling carrots, Mr Struthers. Not in the circumstances.

Nigel: If they link your pay to performance, you might at least try to help.

Nurse: There's only so much I can do, Mr Struthers. After all, we must keep it professional. You're on your own now.

Nurse moves towards the exit and stops to deliver her parting line.

Nurse: Apparently fantasy can be quite effective.

Nigel *(Sarcastically to her back)***:** Thank you so much. Fantasy, she says, fantasy. *(Shouting after her.)* Fantasy's for people who haven't got lives of their own. Like bank clerks and accountants and uptight nurses with woollen knickers who think *Lady in Red* is a masterpiece and Chris de Burgh should be made Pope. It's for people whose lives are so predictable they have to live in some parallel, imaginary universe. It's a kind of mental Sony Playstation.

No, you should give up fantasy the moment you hit puberty, just as soon as you know you're never going to pull on a shirt with the three lions on it. When you know you're never going to be the one who makes that long journey up the steps towards the Royal Box. *(Nigel acts out his words.)* There's the Jules Rimet Trophy, gleaming gold on its little stand. Twelve inches of glittering, glorious gold.

You've got to shake hands with the Queen. You look at them. They're covered with sweat and Wembley turf. You wipe them on your jersey, but they're not clean enough, so you splay them flat and smear them along the velvet edge of the Royal Box and ... but there's no more Wembley ... and anyway, you knew one wet, Thursday afternoon when Spacca Martin nutmegged you in PE and everyone fell about.

Spacca-bloody-Martin, for God's sake. That's why you don't have fantasies. You grow up. It's for kids and people with motiveless lives. And I've got a life. I've got a life and I've got a sex life. Maybe not at the moment, but you're not meant to do it for a week or so beforehand anyway, so even if there was someone, I wouldn't have recently.

But, in principle, I have a sex life. Ask Jenny Threadgold. She'll tell you. That was her trouble. She told everyone. Christ, that was embarrassing. Might as well have put it out on *News at Ten*. All the other post-grads whinnying at me in the corridor. Fantasy! *(Shouts after her again.)* Fantasy! I'll give you fantasy! The last thing I need is someone handing out psychological advice.

Nigel goes back behind the screen and prepares himself for action.

Nigel *(As Tarantino)*: "OK, Mr Pink, let's go to work." *(Half-sings.)* In, out, in, out, shake it all about. You do the hokey-cokey and you turn around and that's what gets results. *(As James Alexander Gordon.)* "Queen of the South 3, Cowdenbeath 2, Struthers versus Penile Tissue - no result."

Nurse returns, but instead of being in uniform, she is dressed in a white laboratory coat and carries a clipboard. She is now in the guise of a psychologist and adopts a Mrs Robinson pose.

Nurse: First sign of madness, Mr Struthers.

Nigel: What?

Nurse: They say it's the first sign of madness - talking to yourself.

Nigel: I wasn't talking to myself. I was talking to ...

Nurse: Yes, Mr Struthers?

Nigel *(Increasingly flustered)*: It may seem a bit silly, but I was actually talking to ... to ... to ... my ...

Nurse: I see, Mr Struthers. A highly-educated man like you and you don't even know what it's called? It beats me why they always ask for intelligent donors.

Nigel: I was talking to my . . .

Nurse: Come on, Mr Struthers, spit it out. You have to face these little fears.

Nigel (*Almost shouts*): Penis!

Nurse: There. That wasn't too hard, was it?

Nigel: Why do you think I was talking to the bloody thing? I don't need your help. I'm fine on my own.

Nurse: Really?

Nigel: Yes, really. I know your sort. All you'll do is ask me some dim questions put together by some loud-mouthed, American socio-path with his own daytime chat show and then tell me I've got an Oedipus complex.

Nurse: And have you, Mr Struthers?

Nigel makes no reply, but wearily starts to do up his trousers again.

Nurse: Just relax, Mr Struthers, lean back, take it easy.

Nurse pushes Nigel, still with his trousers at half-mast onto the couch. She takes the chair, clipboard and pen poised, ready to conduct a talking cure.

Nurse: Have you done this before, Mr Struthers?

Nigel: It's my first time.

Nurse: Really? I thought young men did it all the time.

Nigel: For money. I'm not doing it for fun. I'm doing it for money.

Nurse: Perhaps your motivation for doing this is an area we could explore in more depth.

Nigel: I do not need exploration or motivation and I certainly don't need depth. I need a hard-on.

Nurse: Shall we talk about your anger?

Nigel: Aaaaaargh!

Nurse: Good. Get to the core of your anger. Perhaps you'd like to scream again?

Nigel (*Hisses*): I am not angry. I simply need to get a little sample into a little bottle and I'm having a little difficulty.

Nurse: You need to loosen up a bit. A strict Freudian might be inclined to call you an anal retentive.

Nigel: I expect you think he's marvellous. I bet you go for it all, don't you?

Nurse: Well . . .

Nigel: Let me tell you something about Freud. He only ever had seven patients and he didn't cure a single one of them. It's hogwash for morons who believe anything they're told.

Nurse: I happen to be a Jungian.

Nigel *(Sarcastically)*: Well, that's a relief. A Swiss nutter rather than an Austrian one.

Nurse *(Earnestly)*: The primordial archetypal images of the subconscious play an important part in who and what we are.

Nigel: More psycho babble. Perhaps you should try English.

Nurse: Things are not always as they appear on the surface.

Nigel: Is that the best you can come up with? Sophisticated intellectual theory and all on the National Health. *(He scratches his head, taunting.)* Scratch wood and there's wood underneath.

Nurse: Scratch veneer and you'll find wood underneath as well, Mr Struthers.

Nigel: OK. Let's keep this on the surface. Give it to me straight. I'm not interested in sub-text.

Nurse: I'm here to give you a helping hand.

Nigel: A helping hand? My own isn't good enough? Your Freudian slip's showing below your crisp, white, efficient coat.

Nurse: Not all veneers have the same patina. Maybe you'd rather talk about your family, Mr Struthers? Your mother, for instance.

Nigel: What's the point?

Nurse: It might just relax you?

Nigel: Relax? There's nothing relaxing about my mother. Except for the Valium. *(Resigned.)* If you insist.

Nurse: You're too tense. Take it easy. *(She goes behind him and begins to massage his shoulders.)* How's that?

Nigel: Surprisingly pleasant.

Nurse: Is anything happening?

Nigel: It's very soothing. Very relaxing.

Nurse: Good. Because nothing's going to happen if you're too tense.

Nigel: I'm not tense. Will you stop saying I'm tense.

Nurse: Shh . . . just ree-lax. Think about something nice and pleasant. Conjure up a nice country scene in your mind. Have you done that?

Nigel: Yes . . .

Nurse: What can you see?

Nigel: Cow shit. I'm not a country lover.

Nurse: You're a townie then?

Nigel: Oh, yes. I was born and brought up in the city.

Nurse: Did you live with your mother?

Nigel: Don't go on about my mother all the time - it's no wonder I'm all tensed up. Down a bit, please.

Nurse massages him lower down his back.

Nurse: So, why are you here?

Nigel: Yes, why I'm here in the first place . . . How did I end up here . . . serving no purpose.

Nurse: You do have a purpose. Everybody has a function in life.

Nigel: Function. Dysfunction. Why here . . . why not MacChicken Kingburgers?

Nurse: You couldn't do this in MacChicken Kingburgers. Not even in the toilet. You'd get arrested. Look at poor old George Michael.

Nigel: It's about four pounds an hour there. It's twenty pounds here. Could you do the bottom of my spine?

Nurse: There you go. *(She massages his spine.)* That's not a bad rate. It's the equivalent of five hours at MacChicken Kingburgers.

Nigel: Which is about how long it's taking here. I'm hardly making money hand over fist

Nurse: And your childhood?

Nigel: It was all right. I don't remember a great deal.

Nurse: Did you have brothers and sisters?

Nigel: No. I'm an only child.

Nurse: Friends?

Nigel: Not a lot. I don't mind my own company. I've always been quite solitary.

Nurse: Ideal for a job like this.
Nigel: I did have one particular friend.
Nurse: What was his name?
Nigel: It was a girl, actually.
Nurse: Buttocks?
Nigel: Yes, please.

Nurse begins to massage his buttocks.

Nigel: Linda. It's Spanish for pretty.
Nurse: You do know a lot. How's that?
Nigel: Excellent. I read a lot as a child.
Nurse: And was she?
Nigel: What?
Nurse: Was Linda pretty?
Nigel: I suppose so. I haven't thought about it in years.
Nurse: Did you play together?
Nigel: Actually, quite a lot now I think of it. You see, I used to have the two top rooms all to myself. We would spend hours up there.
Nurse: And did you ever play doctors and nurses?
Nigel: I don't remember. We may have.
Nurse: I bet playing doctors and nurses would get you going. Now let's see. How are we doing?
Nigel: Nothing yet.
Nurse: Ah, well. We've got plenty of time. No-one else needs this cubicle. Is there a Mrs Struthers?
Nigel: Only my mother.
Nurse: So, tell me about your mother.
Nigel: Will you stop going on about my mother?
Nurse: Aha! So you have got an Oedipus complex. I thought we'd get beneath the carapace.
Nigel *(Explodes)*: I haven't got any complexes at all. I do not have a superiority complex, inferiority complex or even, for that matter, a shopping complex. And, above all, and I wish to make this absolutely one hundred percent clear, I do not have an Oedipus complex. Got that? I have absolutely no desire to shag my mother.
Nurse: Your father then?

Nigel: My father's been dead for ten years!

Nurse: It's worse than I thought. Necrophilia.

Nigel: You're mad. Totally, raving, mad. Leave me alone.

> *Nurse is scared off by Nigel's threatening posture and exits hurriedly. Nigel picks up the clipboard and is about to throw it after her, but looks at it instead.*

Nigel: Oh yeah, that's right. Make your handwriting almost illegible so you can pass yourself off as a proper doctor. *(Reads.)* Combative. Angry. Arrogant. Prejudiced against psychotherapy. *(Tosses it away.)* Who do these people think they are? Read a few books by a couple of Germanic loonies and they want to have you locked away. *(As Freud.)* "Oh yes, Carl. Would you believe this? He actually examines his shit after he takes a dump." *(As Jung.)* "Oh, no, Sigmund, you know vot zis means?" *(Freud.)* "Of course, Carl. He's obviously anally fixated. It's going to take years to cure." *(Jung.)* "Ah good, just think of all ze money ve vill make."

(Himself.) Stalinists. Make sure your emotions fit in with the new, caring, sharing totalitarian emotion Nazis. Shit, shit, shit, shit, shit. Shit, I promised my mother I wouldn't swear. They're the pits. Give them a degree in something they only pretend they understand and they're out to get you in the individual cell with nice, extra soft wallpaper and the comfy jackets with the extra long sleeves. *(Germanic accent.)* "Don't worry, Nigel, we'll do them up at the back." *(Himself.)* It was supposed to be an easy twenty quid. Jesus. It's like some kind of weird, satanic nightmare. *(Shouts after Nurse who is long gone.)* Emotional Nazis - that's what you are.

What's wrong with a stiff upper lip? Hey? Upper lip - stiff. Penis - limp. *(Screams.)* Some of us are perfectly capable of keeping our emotions in check. We don't need bloody Shamans to tell us how to feel or think or . . . whatever.

(Sotto voce.) Calm down, my son. Calm down. This isn't going to get you anywhere. *(Nigel lifts away the waistband of his trousers and peers in.)* Limp as a lettuce, limp as a one-legged man. *(In the*

egregious manner of an awards ceremony host.) "And snail of the year goes to Nigel Struthers's willie."
Nurse re-enters, dressed in jodhpurs, riding gear, etc. Inevitably, she carries a riding crop. She is straight out of the pages of Clichéd Dominatrix Monthly.

Nurse: You're bound to get the odd refusal. The best thing is to dismount and lead him round again.

Nigel: Dismount?

Nurse: They're wicked little beasts, aren't they? They've got minds of their own, you know.

Nigel: Maybe that's why they don't work in hospitals.

Nurse: Let me tell you a story, Mr Struthers. *(Nurse runs her riding crop across Nigel's face.)* God creates Adam and he's pleased with his handiwork. And he says to Adam, "Look, I'm going to give you two wonderful organs. One will allow you to think so cleverly, that you'll become more important than all the other animals on the planet. This organ is called the brain. The other will give you the greatest pleasure you will ever know. This organ is called the penis." "Brilliant," says Adam, "What's the catch?" "Well," says God, "You won't be able to use them both at the same time.

Nigel: And what am I supposed to learn from that?

Nurse: You think too much. Some of us prefer action. Time for your riding lesson!
Nurse rams Nigel back onto the couch and straddles him.

Nigel: What the fu . . .

Nurse: You've been ignoring me and I'm a real woman with real needs and real breasts.
She clamps his hands onto her breasts on the outside of her clothing.
Nigel is terrified.

Nigel: So it would seem.

Nurse: I understand your problem. We'll get that little chap back in the saddle in no time at all. Don't be modest. Don't be shy. You're such a man. What's a little horseplay between friends?

Nigel: Well it's awfully . . .
Nurse flops over onto her back in a provocative position.

Nurse: Take me, Mr Struthers. Now, whilst I've got the bit between my teeth.

Nigel: It's a kind offer. It's not that I'm ungrateful.

Nurse: I don't want gratitude. I want to turn you on.

Nigel: How the hell am I supposed to get turned on with some bloody woman touching me up all the time? It's all a bit sudden.

Nurse: Mr Struthers, it may be sudden for you, but I've known since the very first time I saw you that you were the man for me. You're a stud. You're a stallion amongst geldings.

Nigel: It's very kind of you, but I'm not allowed to do it for a week beforehand.

Nurse: It's four points for a refusal, Mr Struthers.

Nigel: And I've never done it with anyone I'm not on first name terms with.

Nurse: On your back, Nigel.

Nurse flips Nigel onto his back again.

Nigel: I meant I had to know their first name.

Nurse: You don't need to know anything. Just take it easy.

Music - "Land of Hope and Glory" starts up in the background.

Nurse: Are you patriotic, Nigel?

Nigel: I like it when we win at football.

Nurse: Lie back and think of England, Nigel. Think of all our triumphs. Germany 1 - England 5. Think of all our achievements. Nothing like a good bit of patriotism, Nigel, for stirring the blood, stiffening the sinew, putting a bit of iron into one's resolve. Have you ever wondered what it might be like to pull on an England jersey, Nigel?

Nigel: Funny you should mention that.

Nurse: The little soldier isn't standing to attention like he should, is he? Think England. Think red, white and blue. Think country. Think Queen. Think pageantry, Albert Hall, the Glorious Twelfth, Ascot, Wimbledon, strawberries and cream, the Saturday of the Lords Test, Henley Regatta, a royal fanfare. We're going to get that flag flying if it's the last thing we do.

Nigel: The National Anthem, The Olympics, the Commonwealth Games, Twickenham and the Six Nations.

Nurse: Good. It's the final of the women's breast-stroke. Sharon Davies, still moist from her triumphant swim, mounts the podium. She's an Amazon, the warrior queen of the water. Her blonde hair is plastered down her back. *(She checks his privates.)* Good, good, good, getting somewhere now. She is strong, svelte, muscled in a feminine way. The official hands her a bunch of flowers and she bows her head, ready to receive the gold medal. That's better, Nigel, amazing what a touch of nationalism can do for the sperm count. Sharon, Nigel, keep the image.

Nurse slips off the couch and exits. Nigel goes behind the screen to carry on his good work. Patriotic music swells . . . it is Jerusalem.

Nigel: Sharon Davies. Village bobby. Crumpets. There is a corner of a foreign field. Thorpe runs it down to third man. Inspector Morse . . . Tower Bridge . . . That's more like it. Getting somewhere now. *(Sings.)* "And did those feet in ancient times, walk upon England's mountains green. And was the holy lamb of God in England's pleasant pastures seen. I shall not cease from mental fight, nor shall my sword sleep in my hand." *(To his penis.)* Not sleeping now are you, son? Patriotism. It's in the blood.

I'm so proud to be English. What a history; what a tradition. Where *we* lead, *others* follow. Look at what we've invented. Football, the seed drill, the clockwork radio, Stan Laurel, cats' eyes, queuing, E-type Jaguar. Better not complain about the service. Monty Python. Hearts of Oak. Getting a plumber at weekends. That's bubbling along nicely now. An Englishman's home is his castle. John Bull. *(In a mummerset accent.)* "How are you, my handsome?" The Trooping of the Colour. Oh, no - that's boring . . . *(Gordon Brown voice.)* "I'm afraid we're just going to have to cope with the consequences of deflation." *(Himself.)* Think English. Boiled cabbage. No, stay up! Please! Yorkshire pudding. English roast beef with English mustard. You snivelling, little, unpatriotic sod.

*Re-enter **Nurse** dressed as a fantasy French Maid, holding a silly fluffy duster and with an outrageous French accent.*

Nurse: Or perhaps you'd prefer a little French mustard? Hey, Nigel?

Nurse walks round the screen and eyes Nigel from head to toe.

Nurse: Ooh, you are a big boy - but you could be bigger still. Maybe a little French tickler.

Nurse tickles Nigel's mid-section with her little feather duster.

Nigel: Where do you come from?

Nurse: France.

Nigel: Why?

Nurse: It's where I come from.

Nigel: How did you get here? Where have you all . . . ?

Nurse: Don't ask such questions. *(She places her finger on Nigel's lips to quieten him. Her eyes are again drawn to his mid-section.)* I'm not here to answer questions. I'm the hand-maid you've been waiting for.

Nigel: I'm confused. You all look so similar.

Nurse: I am your genie.

Nigel (*Holds up his sample bottle***):** You mean you're like the genie of the lamp? You rub the lamp and the genie appears? You're like the genie of bottle?

Nurse: Only it's not the bottle you've been rubbing now, is it, you naughty, naughty boy?

Nurse takes the bottle from him and places it provocatively in her cleavage.

Nigel: You know why I'm here?

Nurse: Of course. And I am here because you need me. French polishing the baguette can be a lonely business.

Nigel: Especially when it's more of a croissant.

Nurse: At times like this, wouldn't you like a bit of French?

Nigel: It's an appetising idea.

Nurse: What kind of French would you like?

Nigel: A French name.

Nurse: It's not important. A French kiss?

Nurse gives him a provocative kiss.

Nigel: I want to know your name.

Nurse: French knickers?

Nigel: It seems wrong otherwise. Animalistic.

Nurse: I'm only here to help. Perhaps a French letter?

Nigel: But without your name?

Nurse: I'm here to get you started. How can I explain this to you? I'm like John the Baptist, preparing the way for the one who will come after me. You can take care of yourself. You're a big boy now. A *very* big boy!

Nigel: You're the only one who's helped.

Nurse: I've been helping all along.

Nigel: What do you mean?

Nurse: It's like donating sperm, Nigel. Sometimes you've just got to work it out for yourself. Rôsbif et moutarde française. French leave.

> *Nurse exits, blowing Nigel an exaggerated kiss from the side.*

Nigel: Wow. She's fantastic. Of course, they've got a long tradition of them. Brigitte Bardot . . . Catherine Deneuve . . . Juliette Binoche . . . Audrey Tatou.

What a woman. What a goddess. It's like a religious experience. It's like Saint Paul on the road to Damascus, when suddenly he sees the light . . . Only that made him go blind. *(Peers in his trousers and is impressed by what he sees.)* Oh well, sometimes it's worth the risk. *(He looks a bit more.)* Attention!

I want you to have my babies and I'm going to start practising now. *(Moves back behind the screen to finish his business.)* Un, deux, trois! Look at the effect you're having on me. Only you can do this to me. English roast beef with French mustard. Thorpe runs the ball down to ding-da-ding da-ding-da-ding *(he does the zither theme from* The Third Man.*)* . . . Well, my little enfant terrible, England expects that today every man shall do his duty. *(Dam Busters March begins.)* Cheddar Gorge . . . Camembert . . . An Englishman's home is his chateau . . . cul-de-sac, gauloise filtre. Je t'adore. Chocolat chaud . . .getting chauder and chauder . . .

As Nigel nears the end, The Dam Busters March *swells to a climax.*

Nigel: Yes. Yes. Oui. Oui. Oui. Coup de grace!

> *Re-enter Nurse in her original nurse's outfit.*
> *She holds out the little sample bottle.*

NIGEL'S WRIST

Nigel: My bottle. Where's the bottle? Oh no! Where's my bottle. I want my bottle.

Nurse: Never mind, Nigel. No use crying over spilled . . .

Nigel: Oh, no. I'm going to have to go through all that again. It's so humiliating.

Nurse: You know the rules, Mr Struthers. You can't do it for at least seven days. You'll just have to come back in a week.

Nigel: A week. But what am I going to do for a week?

Nurse: Perhaps you should develop some other hobbies, Mr Struthers.

Nigel: A week?

Nurse: A week.

Nigel: Can I have the same day and time - only it fits in with other commitments.

Nurse: Certainly, Mr Struthers. Anything else?

Nigel: Yes. Next time I'd like Doris Day, *Ride of the Valkyries* and the PE mistress.

Nurse: No problem.

Nigel: See you next week then.

Nurse: See you next week, then.

Nigel exits, putting on his jacket. Nurse watches him go.

Nurse: Wanker!

Curtain